Molly Meacher,

CLASS 2 TEACHER

Written by Jonny Zucker

Illustrated by Kelly Canby

OXFORD
UNIVERSITY PRESS

OXFORD
UNIVERSITY PRESS

Great Clarendon Street, Oxford, OX2 6DP, United Kingdom

Oxford University Press is a department of the University
of Oxford. It furthers the University's objective of excellence
in research, scholarship, and education by publishing
worldwide. Oxford is a registered trade mark of Oxford
University Press in the UK and in certain other countries

Text © Jonny Zucker 2015
Illustrations © Oxford University Press 2015

The moral rights of the author have been asserted

First published 2015

British Library Cataloguing in Publication Data
Data available

ISBN: 978-0-19-835669-1

10 9 8 7 6 5 4

Paper used in the production of this book is a natural, recyclable product
made from wood grown in sustainable forests. The manufacturing process
conforms to the environmental regulations of the country of origin.

Printed in China by Leo Paper Products Ltd

Acknowledgements

Series Advisor: Nikki Gamble
Illustrated by Kelly Canby

Chapter 1
Classroom Chaos

"Alvin Lee. Stop spinning around in that chair!
Zara Smith. Stop pulling Ned's ears! Yasmin
Sharma. Stop bouncing that ball!"

Miss Molly Meacher was trying to control her
class at Hill Top Primary School.

"The next person to misbehave will have no
playtime on Friday," said Molly.

Alvin stopped spinning. Zara let go of Ned's ears. Yasmin dropped the ball.

"Good," said Molly. "Now I can teach you how to play this game."

"I'm going to be the best," smirked Alvin.

"I'll be way better," said Yasmin.

"No, Alvin, hold the controller this way up!" Molly sighed.

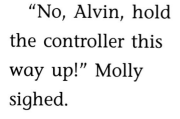

"Yasmin, don't open the disc drive with a ruler!"

"Miss Meacher," called Ned, "this is harder than that mini tablet thing you showed us."

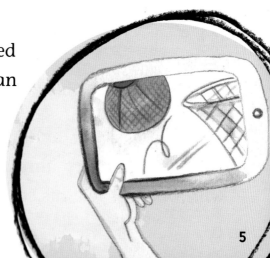

Molly Meacher was just like any other teacher, except for one thing: she was eight years old.

The real teachers of Hill Top Primary were away on a training course. So for one week, the children were being the teachers and the children's parents were being the pupils.

It was Day One and Molly was exhausted. Her class was very unruly, especially Alvin Lee, who was just like his son, Freddie.

At that moment, the headteacher, Mr Robert Kenton (aged ten), wheeled into Molly's classroom.

"Miss Meacher," he smiled. "I have something for you and your students."

He handed Molly an envelope.

"Is it money?" shouted Alvin, who worked in a bank.

"Is it football tickets?" cried Yasmin, who ran a sports shop.

Molly opened the envelope.

"It's an invitation to enter a biscuit-making competition," she said. "The winners will take part in a live TV final with baking expert, Abby Jansen."

"*Awesome!*" the class squealed.

"I love Abby Jansen!" Alvin declared.

"I buy her cookbooks and bake her cakes for my children!" gushed Yasmin.

Chapter 2
Kitchen Antics

"I'm not sure this class is ready for a competition," frowned Molly.

"Oh *please*, Miss!" begged the adults.

"We'll be amazing!" called Alvin, straightening his tie.

"We'll be perfect," said Zara, giving Molly her most winning smile.

"You could make some biscuits in your cooking class tomorrow," Mr Kenton reminded her.

"Oh … OK," Molly sighed. "But I want everyone on their best behaviour!"

"YAY!" yelled the adults.

The next morning, Molly's
class brought in the ingredients
for biscuit-making.

Yasmin Sharma's daughter, Leela, was talking
to her mother. "Do what Miss Meacher says,"
she fussed, "and don't make a mess. Remember
that soup you spilled last week?"

"Yes, daughter," sighed Yasmin.

"Miss Fipps is kindly letting us use the school
kitchen before she arrives at 10 o'clock," Molly
told her class.

Miss Carol Fipps (aged eleven) was in charge of the kitchen. She was already turning out to be the meanest person in the school. She certainly wouldn't like to find adults making a mess in 'her' kitchen!

"Use these basic biscuit recipes," said Molly when they were ready to start. "Then add to them to make some new and wonderful biscuits."

"Once we win, I'm going to sell my biscuits and make **millions**," boasted Alvin.

"I'm going to use mine as sports snacks," said Yasmin.

Before long some amazing biscuits were taking shape, but the kitchen was a complete mess.

Molly was so busy that when she looked at the clock, she got a big shock. Miss Fipps would be arriving in two minutes!

"Quickly, everyone," shouted Molly. "We need to clean this place up. *Now!*"

"Leave it to me!" shouted Ned, who ran a cleaning company. But at that very second the kitchen door burst open with a loud

BANG!

Chapter 3
The Biscuit Rescue

In walked Miss Fipps.

"In my two days of working here, I have never seen such a disgraceful mess!" she snarled.

"Get out!"

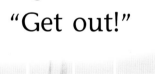

"B ... b ... but what about our biscuits?" asked Alvin, with jam dripping down his cheek.

Miss Fipps pulled the half-baked biscuits out of the oven and slammed them down on a table. Lots of them broke.

"I said *get out!*"

Class 2 grumbled as they walked out to the playground for break-time.

Back in her classroom, Molly was washing her hands when Miss Fipps stormed in.

"I crushed your horrible biscuit inventions and shoved them in here," she told Molly, slamming a big plastic container on Molly's desk and stomping out.

Molly knew that her class would be
incredibly upset if they saw the broken
biscuits, so she quickly hid the container
in the Class 2 cupboard.

"Where are our biscuits?" panted Alvin
as he ran in from break-time.

"They're … er … they're fine," stammered
Molly. "I'm looking after them."

After school that day, Alvin's son, Freddie, came to speak to Molly.

"Dad is *so* excited about this biscuit competition," he told Molly. "He really thinks your class can make it to the TV final."

"Let's hope so," blushed Molly.

The next morning, Molly was horrified to see the Class 2 cupboard open.

The biscuit container was gone.

"Oh, hi Miss," came a voice from across the room.

Alvin and Yasmin were sitting at a table and they had the missing container!

"You shouldn't have opened my cupboard," scolded Molly.

"We wanted a hot drink," explained Yasmin, "and we found a tin of coffee inside."

"We also found this container," added Alvin.

"I ... I ... I ..." spluttered Molly.

"We were upset at first but then we had an idea," said Yasmin.

"We stuck some of the broken bits together with icing and made this mega biscuit," said Alvin.

He held up a beautiful creation. It was brown and pink and yellow, with three layers and a smooth cream filling.

"Wow!" gasped Molly. "That really *is* a mega biscuit!"

Chapter 4
Lights, Camera, Action!

When the other adults saw the mega biscuit, they went wild with delight.

"I need to fill out the competition entry form and include a photo of our biscuit," said Molly.

She borrowed Yasmin's mobile phone and took a close-up snap.

At lunchtime she emailed the form and photo to the competition organizers.

An hour later an email came back.

"The email says," announced Molly, "that our school entry has made it to the final. And the final is *tomorrow!*"

"We're going to be on TV!" the adults screamed with joy.

The next day, Molly and her class took a bus to the TV studio.

Molly was asked to pick two pupils. Those two would go up on stage to show the mega biscuit when it was Hill Top's turn.

"Pick me, pick me!" shouted Alvin.

"You *did* fix the biscuit, Alvin," replied Molly. "So you and Yasmin can go up on stage."

"I'm going to be a TV star!" Alvin whooped, texting several of his friends with the news.

Suddenly, the lights went down and famous
TV chef Abby Jansen walked onto the stage.
Everyone clapped and cheered, especially Alvin.

"Welcome, everyone!" declared Abby. "May the best biscuit win!"

One by one, children from the other schools went up on stage with their biscuits.

"When is it Hill Top's turn?" whispered Alvin every few seconds.

"Soon," shushed Molly every few seconds.

Finally, it was Alvin and Yasmin's turn.

Chapter 5
The Big Biscuit Moment

They scrambled onto the stage, Alvin gingerly holding their mega biscuit.

"Who have we got here?" asked Abby.

Alvin giggled nervously. Yasmin nudged him. Alvin giggled some more. Yasmin shoved him.

Alvin fell forwards and the biscuit went all over Abby's jacket. Furious, Abby stormed off the stage.

"Alvin should stick to *banking*, not baking!" groaned Yasmin, as she and Alvin left the stage. The whole class glared at Alvin.

"I'm sorry," he mumbled.

Ten minutes later, Abby reappeared wearing a different jacket.

"I've now tasted every biscuit," she announced, "and the winner is ..."

Everyone in the TV studio held their breath.

"… the one that I had to *wear on my jacket!* It was delicious!"

"**We've won!**" the Hill Top adults cheered.

Alvin, Yasmin and Molly were invited onto the stage. Abby presented Molly with a gold trophy and a silver envelope.

The next morning, Molly's students were racing around the playground, celebrating.

Amazingly, Miss Fipps was out celebrating with them, too. The competition prize money was going to be used to fix the school kitchen!

Molly and Mr Kenton watched the scene from the side of the playground.

"So, Molly," said Mr Kenton, "have you enjoyed being a teacher?"

"Yes," replied Molly, "but my class has been pretty rowdy."

"Especially Alvin," nodded Mr Kenton.

"It *has* been fun ordering them around," added Molly, "but I'm exhausted."

"It'll all be over soon," smiled Mr Kenton. "On Monday we'll be pupils again."

"You know, I think there are some pieces of the mega biscuit left," said Molly.

"Race you for them!" yelled Mr Kenton.

Molly grinned and the two of them sped into the staffroom, watched by a playground full of very surprised adults.